Printed in Great Britain
by Amazon

34412933R00069